Rookie Read-About® Science

Acorn to Oak Tree

by Lisa M. Herrington

Content Consultant

Elizabeth Case DeSantis, M.A. Elementary Education
Julia A. Stark Elementary School, Stamford, Connecticut

Reading Consultant

Jeanne M. Clidas, Ph.D.
Reading Specialist

Children's Press®
An Imprint of Scholastic Inc.
New York Toronto London Auckland Sydney
Mexico City New Delhi Hong Kong
Danbury, Connecticut

Library of Congress Cataloging-in-Publication Data
Herrington, Lisa M.
  Acorn to oak tree/by Lisa M. Herrington; content consultant Elizabeth Case DeSantis,
M.A. Elementary Education, Grade 2 Teacher, Julia A. Stark Elementary, Stamford,
Connecticut; reading consultant, Jeanne Clidas, Ph.D.
    pages cm. — (Rookie read-about science)
  Includes index.
  Audience: Age 3 - 6.
  ISBN 978-0-531-21054-3 (library binding) — ISBN 978-0-531-24975-8 (pbk.)
1. Oak—Life cycles—Juvenile literature. 2. Acorns—Juvenile literature. I. Title.

  QK495.F14H45 2014
  583'.46—dc23   2013034812

Produced by Spooky Cheetah Press
Design by Keith Plechaty

© 2014 by Scholastic Inc.

Printed in China 62

SCHOLASTIC, CHILDREN'S PRESS, ROOKIE READ-ABOUT®, and associated logos are
trademarks and/or registered trademarks of Scholastic Inc.

1 2 3 4 5 6 7 8 9 10 R 23 22 21 20 19 18 17 16 15 14

Photographs © 2014: Alamy Images: cover top right, 12, 27 bottom, 31 center bottom
(Clint Farlinger), 29 left inset (Gale S. Hanratty), 23 (shapencolour); Getty Images: 4
(danleap), 29 left (Gary Vestal), 16 (Howard Rice/Garden Picture Library); iStockphoto/
Kasom: 30; Minden Pictures/Colin Varndell/NPL: 19; Science Source: 28 inset (Harry
Rogers), 24 (Jeffrey Lepore), 29 right inset (Ken Brate), 20 (Kenneth Murray), 15, 26
bottom (Leonard Lee Rue III), 8, 31 center top (Michael P. Gadomski), 29 right (Norm
Thomas), cover top left, 7, 26 top, 31 top (Richard Parker); Shutterstock, Inc./kosam:
cover bottom; Superstock, Inc.: 28 (age fotostock), cover top center, 11, 27 top, 31
bottom (imagebroker.net); Thinkstock: 3 bottom (Hemera), 3 top (iStockphoto).

Table of Contents

Oak Tree

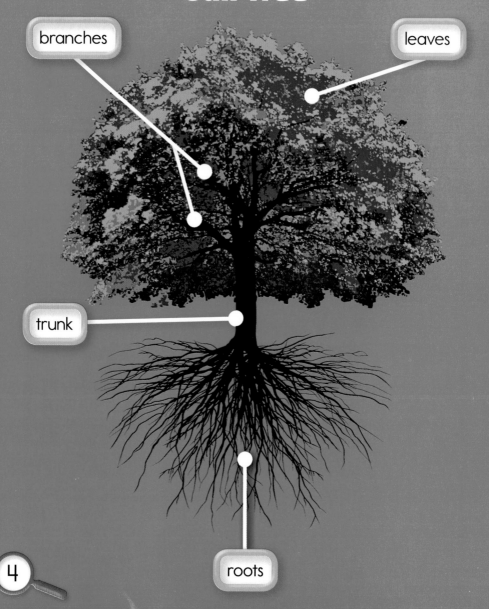

branches

leaves

trunk

roots

Mighty Oaks

Trees are made up of four parts: **roots**, trunk, branches, and leaves. An oak tree is one type of tree. It can grow very tall. Some mighty oaks live to be more than 400 years old!

Acorns grow on an oak's branches.

An oak tree's life begins with an **acorn**. Acorns are the seeds of an oak tree. Inside the acorn's hard shell is the seed.

Oak trees grow from acorns. Other trees grow from different types of seeds.

roots

In fall, acorns drop to the ground. In spring, an acorn's shell cracks open. A tiny root pushes out of the shell and down into the soil.

The root brings water and food up from the soil.

The stem brings water up from the root to other parts of the tree.

Growing Up

A small **shoot**, or stem, pushes up from the acorn. Tiny leaves unfold on the shoot.

FUN FACT!

Some oaks can grow to more than 130 feet (40 meters) tall!

leaves

stem

sapling

The small shoot grows into a young tree. It is called a **sapling**. The tree has very thin branches and just a few leaves.

This sapling grows toward the sunlight.

The tiny acorn has grown into a big oak tree!

Each year, the tree grows bigger and bigger. More leaves appear. The tree's trunk and branches become thicker.

FUN FACT!

An oak's strong wood is used to make furniture and floors. It was once used to build ships.

15

Seasons of Change

In fall, most oak leaves change colors. The leaves then drop to the ground.

This oak tree's leaves have turned red. Other oak leaves turn yellow or orange.

In spring, buds form on the branches of the tree. New leaves will open from the buds.

These buds have new leaves inside.

In summer, flowers grow on adult oak trees. The flowers are called catkins. They help the tree make new acorns.

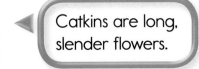

Catkins are long, slender flowers.

The Cycle Continues

By fall, new acorns are grown. Soon, they will fall off the tree.

A fully grown oak tree can produce more than 50,000 acorns!

A squirrel gathers acorns for winter.

Squirrels, birds, and deer eat many acorns. Some lucky acorns grow roots. An oak tree's life cycle begins again.

About one out of every 10,000 acorns will become an oak tree.

An Oak Tree's

An oak tree grows from a seed called an acorn.

About 20 years later, the oak is an adult. Its flowers make new acorns.

Life Cycle

Think About It

What is the seed of an oak tree called?

What happens to an acorn as it grows?

How does an oak tree make new acorns?

In spring, the acorn grows a root into the ground. A shoot pushes upward.

The shoot grows into a young tree called a sapling.

Outstanding

The oak is the national tree of the United States. Oak trees are found across the country. They also live in other parts of the globe. There are about 500 kinds of oak trees in the world. All oak trees come from acorns.

white oak acorns

White oaks have leaves with round, fingerlike edges.

Oaks

live oak acorns

black oak acorns

Blacks oaks have pointy leaves with thin tips.

Live oaks get their name because their leaves stay green in winter. They grow mainly in southern parts of the United States.

Let's Explore!

Go on a nature hunt for acorns and oak trees. Keep a journal and drawings of what you see. What do the leaves, trunk, and bark look like? Do you see any acorns or flowers on the tree? Do you notice any wildlife? If so, what is it doing? Return to the same spot and draw the tree in different seasons. How has it changed? Why, do you think, did the changes happen?

Food Chain

Living creatures depend on each other for their food. Trees help animals grow and move through their own life cycles. Small animals use trees or their seeds for food. Then many small animals become food for larger animals. This is called a food chain.

Acorn

An acorn falls from an oak tree.

Squirrel

A squirrel eats the acorn.

Coyote

A coyote then eats the squirrel. Other animals that prey on squirrels include foxes and great horned owls.

Glossary

acorn (AY-korn): the seed of an oak tree

roots (ROOTS): the parts of a tree that grow underground and take in water and food from the soil

sapling (SAP-ling): a young tree

shoot (SHOOT): the first stem and leaves of a plant just above the soil

Index

Facts for Now

Visit this Scholastic Web site for more information on oak trees:
www.factsfornow.scholastic.com
Enter the keywords **Oak Trees**

About the Author

Lisa M. Herrington writes books and articles for kids. She lives in Trumbull, Connecticut, with her husband, Ryan, and daughter, Caroline. Growing up, she spent her summers reading books and seeking shade under the tall oak trees in her grandparents' yard.